MY
KENTUCKY
LIFE

ISBN 978-1-935497-67-7

Book design by Carly Schnur

Cover image of the author, Dave Shuffett,
and his current television co-host, Toby, by Madi Bates

Endsheet image of the meteorite crater in Middlesboro, Kentucky
by Dave Shuffett

Unless otherwise noted, all photographs in this book
were taken by and are copyright © Dave Shuffett

Printed in Canada

Published by:
Butler Books
P.O. Box 7311
Louisville, KY 40257
Phone (502) 897-9393
Fax (502) 897-9797

www.butlerbooks.com

MY KENTUCKY LIFE

DAVE SHUFFETT

To Sandy, my one and only,
for sharing my Kentucky life

INTRODUCTION

That summer night in the Colorado Rockies is one I'll never forget. I was camped alone at 9,000 feet. Normally I would have retreated to a hotel or lodge by dark. But on this night I had decided to rough it alone, just for the experience. I thought I had seen bright stars before, but none like this. Not even thoughts of bears could distract me from what I was seeing. At that altitude, the clear air without light pollution was giving me a show to top all night-sky shows. The Milky Way looked as if I could reach up and touch it, and it surely contained more stars than there are numbers. As shooting stars raced across the heavens every few minutes, words from the John Denver song came to mind: "And the Colorado Rocky Mountain high, I've seen it rainin' fire in the sky."

By the summer of 1998 and by the age of 40, I had crisscrossed Colorado, Wyoming, Utah, California, and Arizona, and more excursions were in the planning stages. My Kentucky home was far behind me now, and I had begun to believe I had found my place on this earth. I was awestruck with the vastness and raw beauty of the great American West—and since I was a toddler I had been fascinated with the cowboy and his way of life. I had even attempted, and I stress attempted, bareback bronco riding in a small rodeo circuit back East in my younger and wilder days.

Now I was producing an outdoor adventure television series that was aired nationally by a cable network and broadcast stations, and it required that I travel the whole country.

My life had become one continuing adventure. I would walk alone across the salt flats of Death Valley, dehydrated from not carrying enough water in 115 degree heat. I would fly-fish the high streams in Wyoming's Wind River Range, hike spectacular trails 12,000 feet high in Colorado's Rocky Mountain National Park, and ride everything under the shining sun. I felt the wind in my face generated from snowmobiles, four-wheelers, horses, and dog sleds.

I'd had ocean adventures, too, and some of them didn't go so well. I was caught in two storms in the Pacific. One hair-raising overnight trip to Channel Islands National Park off the coast of California surely looked similar to the opening scenes of the old TV series "Gilligan's Island." Even the crew got seasick. And a night fishing trip off San Diego turned sour when our trawler was nearly beaten to death by large waves from an unexpected storm. We turned back and made it safely to San Diego, somehow.

Sponsors paid the bills, but these adventures were often "trade outs." In exchange for some publicity on my show, national park concessioners, guide services of all kinds, and guest ranches were happy to host me free of charge. Even getting there was sometimes a trade out. On one occasion Amtrak gave my videographer and me first-class accommodations from Cincinnati to Chicago and on to Denver. From there we rented a four-wheel-drive truck and set out on another trip to Wyoming. Within hours I was in the saddle for the third time, riding alongside guest ranch owner and cowgirl Kinta Blumenthal. She and her husband often joked that "you can get the boy out of Kentucky, but not the Kentucky out of the boy."

That joking remark is quite true. You can't get the Kentucky out of the boy. My family joined me when they could, but not nearly enough. I missed them and I missed the state I grew up in. I missed the hazy sunsets of summer, tobacco patches, cattle and horses grazing in green, rolling hills—and I missed the people that make Kentucky so special.

In 1999, I returned to my place of familiarity. As I had done before, I would set out on a continuing journey as a writer and television producer of all things Kentucky— and over the years I have been fortunate enough to see the greatest places and meet the greatest people our state has to offer.

This book is a compilation of stories and photographs spanning 25 years of travel in Kentucky. I consider myself a storyteller. I took up still photography later in life and found that it's an entirely different learning process from videography. But wherever I go across Kentucky, I am hardly ever without my digital camera.

There are too many pictures and stories for one book, so I'm calling this one Volume One of a series. No region of the state will be left out as I continue my travels and complete more books.

As still photography goes, I owe a lot to photographer Steve Shaffer. Steve is one of the best in the business, and over the years he's answered my questions and repeatedly shown his virtue of patience through my learning process.

These days computers enable us to do just about anything we want to with photographs. We can correct major mistakes. We can turn a dull, gray sky into turquoise blue and put in puffy white clouds. None of my photographs have been through enhancement of that nature. In this book you'll see what I saw. You may notice that I appear in a few of the photographs. They were either done by tripod and time exposure, or by me placing the settings where I wanted and handing the camera to someone to take the picture.

As for the stories, I'm an old hand at telling those. So between the two, I hope this book brings smiles and pride in a state that is full of wonder and uniqueness.

KENTUCKY'S NATURAL WONDERS

Even as a young boy I was a wilderness explorer. I would often disappear into the woods behind our house, imagining I was a famous pioneer like Daniel Boone. I would seek out the unknown: perhaps a piece of ground no human had ever walked upon, or maybe an unexplored cave. And I would come home with treasures that my parents begrudgingly tolerated—rocks of all kinds, hiking sticks from downed limbs, occasional critters ranging from snakes to turtles—and always dirt from head to toe.

Ike Durham, a friend of the family, often saw me in that condition and began calling me "little Mudcat." It stuck to me like glue, and within a few years everyone I knew in Green County, including relatives, called me Mudcat. My nickname became so prevalent that folks began using easy, shortened versions of it like "Cat" or "Mud." This was quite the unusual name for a self-proclaimed outdoor adventurer, but I had no choice but to smile and live with it, though I would often dream of having a nickname as grand as "Buffalo Bill." How lucky he was. Years would pass and my first gray hairs and wrinkles would appear before I finally got used to turning my head when someone called me by my real name, David. But I will always be Mudcat back home, a nickname that came as a result of traipsing through forest and field and getting up close and personal with Mother Earth.

I probably inherited my love of the outdoors from my father, Billy Shuffett, an outdoorsman himself and an avid Green River fisherman. He took me on unforgettable float trips aboard his flat-bottomed wooden jon-boat. He was a

Morning sunshine shimmers through the canopy of an eastern Kentucky forest.

laid-back, patient fisherman, the opposite of Uncle Tommy Skaggs, who would often accompany us on these river fishing trips. Tommy was a fidgety fellow, always tripping over tackle boxes and sticking hooks in his fingers. But he could catch fish with the best of them, and he was interested in seeing me become a good fisherman, too. I remember Tommy scolding me on one float trip when I was seven or eight years old. "Mudcat, I've told you to get your lure over closer to the bank where the rocks and the root wads are," he berated, wrapping his bleeding thumb in a handkerchief. Dad just smiled and didn't say anything. But I listened. Focusing now on the task at hand, I cast my Heddon River Runt (a popular river fishing lure of the time) toward the bank and watched it land right next to a root wad. Within seconds a decent smallmouth bass took it! I couldn't believe it was really happening. Before this day I didn't have but two or three small bluegills in my fishing portfolio. I remember feeling both elation and anxiety as I reeled in the fish while Dad and Tommy yelled, "That a boy!" "Nice fish!" I relive that day every time I return to that old river. And I can hear them as plain as day, their voices echoing off the cliffs from somewhere downstream, just out of reach.

Dad was my greatest hero, but Uncle Tommy came in a close second, so it was only fitting that I named my son William Thomas.

It seems as if I floated Green River a thousand times before I was 12 years old. I remember playful grey squirrels bounding along the limbs of old sycamore trees, the noble stance of a great blue heron degraded by his obnoxious call, the upside-down mirrored images of boulders reflecting off the water—and I recall the fight of nearly every river smallmouth I ever caught. Much of my youth was spent in the woods or on the water, early experiences that had such a profound impact that I doubt if I will ever get them out of my system.

Nothing man-made will ever stir my soul like a clear blue day in the great outdoors. And if heaven is a city made of gold, I don't know if I want to go. I'd rather have a cabin by a creek, where dogs still get ticks and the fish don't always bite.

The cool, inviting falls of Bell County's Shillalah Creek in mid-summer

When I paddle a remote stream or walk in the deep woods, I experience a reconnection with old truths buried somewhere in all of us. Perhaps I am sensing the memories of our ancient ancestors who were one with the natural world, not occasional participants. Like them, I am very much aware of what's around me. I take a deep breath and inhale the smell of life in the forest. My physical and emotional being is invigorated, and I am keenly aware of the difference between this and its opposite—lazily reclining on a couch in front of a television. As I gaze up and see the sun's rays shimmering down through the forest canopy, I feel alive.

I've always longed to be away from civilization as often as modern society will allow. In my career, I found ways to escape frequently to the wilderness and still earn an income, in recent years as an outdoor adventure writer for *Kentucky Living* magazine and host of KET's "Kentucky Life."

LESSONS OF THE WILDERNESS

If you spend a lot of time in remote areas as I do, a multitude of things can go wrong if you're not prepared. Feelings of invigoration can turn to feelings of trepidation in an instant. That's what happened to Craig Caudill.

On a cold day in the late fall of 1982, Craig, then 13, began to run wildly through the forest in a state of panic. He had entered the Daniel Boone National Forest on a quest for deer, but quickly lost the trail he came in on because he was hyper-focused on hunting. Panic-stricken and in a blind run, Craig started shedding his outer clothing because he had gotten hot. Fortunately, after being lost all day, he stumbled on a trail that led to a road, and eventually home. But he had done everything wrong, from a directionless run to shedding his outerwear, which could have led to hypothermia in the cold of November.

That experience was life altering for the young hunter. As he grew older, Craig learned everything he could about wilderness survival and becoming a good woodsman. He read dozens of books and articles, trained with experts, and twice went into the wilderness for 30 days with nothing but a knife and lived to tell about it. Surviving in the summer wasn't so hard. But when he tried it in the dead of winter, he says, "It really, really put me to the test." In all of his wilderness education he also learned how lucky he was to have lived through that terrible situation when he was a boy. He could have run in circles and, after finally becoming exhausted, frozen to death. It happens all too often in wilderness areas across the country.

In 2006 Craig created the Nature Reliance School, based in Winchester, Kentucky. He conducts programs in schools for kids and weekend classes out in the woods. I took one of those classes. I was amazed at what I had in my pack that would do me

Craig Caudill uses a fire striker to light a campfire.

no good if I got lost. Even cell phones and GPS devices can be unreliable because they depend on batteries.

Craig teaches people the rule of threes. You can only last three hours without maintaining core body temperature, three days without water, and three weeks without food. The contents of a daypack or backpack should include a tarp for shelter, fire-starting supplies, flashlights, a water purification device, a compass, and a knife larger than a folding pocketknife. Craig also teaches people how to build lean-to shelters and other fundamentals of wilderness survival.

From his near tragedy as a teenager, Craig has created something good that can help all of us who use and love the great outdoors.

Chained Rock at Pine Mountain State Resort Park. In 1933, in an attempt to boost tourism in the area, local residents hauled a 100-foot-long chain by mule team up a mountain "to keep the rock from falling on Pineville directly below." It was a publicity stunt that worked. The hike out to Chained Rock is still a popular destination for tourists visiting the state park.

WHAT WE HAVE

Our remaining wild areas include the Daniel Boone National Forest, with its 707,000 acres of rugged eastern Kentucky highlands and 3,400 miles of sandstone cliffs. Out to the west is the Land Between the Lakes National Recreation Area (commonly referred to as LBL) with 170,000 acres and 300 miles of undeveloped shoreline along Kentucky and Barkley lakes. Of the state's original 1.5 million acres of wetlands, 300,000 acres of these important wildlife habitats remain, most of them in far western Kentucky along the Ohio and Mississippi rivers. We have five areas in the National Park System, including one that is a household name—Mammoth Cave National Park. Kentucky's designated state wild and scenic rivers include sections of the Cumberland, the Rockcastle, and the Big South Fork of the Cumberland, and the Red River has its own designation as a National Wild and Scenic River. We also have bragging rights to some of the finest little gems in the country, the state parks. In all, Kentucky has 52 state parks, including 17 specially designated "state resort parks" with lodging and restaurants.

In the East, Breaks Interstate Park, which straddles the border of Kentucky and Virginia, offers visitors splendid views of one of the deepest gorges in the eastern US and the white water of the Russell Fork of the Big Sandy River at the bottom. In the West, the giant twin lakes, Kentucky Lake and Lake Barkley, boast great fishing and boating opportunities. They are so big that when you look down the middle of either of them, it looks more like an ocean than a lake because you can't see land. I've stayed at Lake Barkley State Resort Park, Kenlake State Resort Park, and Kentucky Dam Village State Resort Park more times than I can remember.

TRAIL #9

One example of the beauty of our state parks can be found at Cumberland Falls State Resort Park and a trail there with an uninspiring name that will leave you inspired. I think it is one of the most breathtaking walks in Kentucky.

The hard, strong rock layers at the site of Cumberland Falls were more difficult for stream water to erode over the millions of years than the softer layers just below the falls. That's why there is a drop—and it's impressive in anyone's book. At 125 feet wide and dropping 65 feet, the falls are the largest in Kentucky and aptly nicknamed "the Niagara of the South." On a sunny day a rainbow may appear in the mist created by the roaring falls. The moonbow is another reason Cumberland Falls is known worldwide. On clear nights during a full moon, a white arc appears over the falls, the result of moonlight shining through the mist. It is the only place in the western hemisphere where a moonbow occurs on a regular basis.

Some of the best views of the falls are along a trail with an unassuming name, Trail #9. This trail offers some of the most scenic vistas our state has to offer. I've walked it dozens of times and I'm still amazed by what I see. The trail begins along highway 90, across the Cumberland River from the park's visitor center. Hikers soon realize how close they are to the top of the falls when they hear its roar just off to the right. This mile and a half, moderately strenuous trail then takes hikers uphill to the highest views of the falls at just under 1,000 feet in elevation.

Up here is where I'm proudest to be a Kentuckian, because these vistas cannot be topped anywhere in America, in my opinion—and I have seen much of America. From here the trail begins to wind its way downhill to the gem at the end, Eagle Falls.

A view of Cumberland Falls
from Trail #9.

The 44-foot-tall Eagle Falls is the gem
at the end of Trail #9.

If the views of Cumberland Falls weren't enough, the end of the trail will put you into another world. The 44-foot-tall Eagle Falls is mesmerizing. I've often stood at the base of these falls and thought, "I could be in Costa Rica." The boulders, the flora, and the clear, inviting pools of water at the bottom of the falls make me think of old Esther Williams movies in tropical paradises.

There is no bad time of year to hike any of the trails at Cumberland Falls State Resort Park, including winter. Without summer foliage, the huge rock formations along the trails and on the river reveal themselves in all their glory. It's far less crowded in the fall and winter. If you hike the trails on the 4th of July you'll be saying "howdy" and sweating a lot. When I come here in the cooler months, I find dramatic views and no distractions to keep me from thinking how lucky I am to be alive.

THE LONGEST CAVE

When you drive or hike through the more than 50,000 "surface acres" of Mammoth Cave National Park, another world is out of sight. Below your feet is the world's longest known cave. In fact, nothing on the planet comes close to its length. So far, 400 miles have been mapped, but no one knows where the cave system finally ends. Park scientists believe it could go on for a whopping 1,000 miles. Retired chief interpreter Mike Adams told me, "You can be driving on top of this cave for six miles before you ever get to the national park boundaries. The cave system is so large it's hard to get your mind around it."

The cave was created by water seeping into limestone strata over millions of years. I compare it to a plate of spaghetti beneath the surface; a labyrinth of corridors looping back and forth and on top of each other. Some of the "rooms" are the size of football fields, and larger. Tours that highlight The Frozen Niagara, Mammoth Dome at 192 feet high, The Grand Avenue, The River Styx, The Bottomless Pit, and Fat Man's Misery expose the beauty of the cave and its bizarre formations. Millions of people can recall that moment when their guide turned out the lights and they found themselves in genuine total darkness for the first time in their lives.

One tour I embarked upon is not for the faint of heart or those with claustrophobia. It's called The Wild Cave Tour. Here an expert park service caver leads "type A" adventurers into tight squeezes with names like "the birth canal." In one area, I pulled myself, chest up, through a hole so small—only nine inches high—that people above a certain size are not allowed to try it. I had to push and pull with all

◀ *The author gazes up at the formations in the Frozen Niagara section of Mammoth Cave.*

A KET television crew shoots pictures and video of the author squeezing through
a narrow section of The Wild Cave Tour.

of my strength to get through. As I paused to catch my breath, it began to dawn
on me that countless tons of limestone were just a couple of inches from my nose.
Because of my experience as a caver, I wasn't terrified, but I was darned glad to get
out of that hole.

Park Service Guides have led visitors into the maze of passageways since Mammoth
Cave became a National Park in 1941. But guiding had been going on long before
that. In the storied history of guiding at Mammoth Cave, the most revered was
a slave named Stephen Bishop, introduced to the cave in 1838. Bishop's owner,
Franklin Gorin, brought Bishop to the cave to work as a guide. Although Bishop
called it a "dark, gloomy and peculiar place," he perhaps felt a sense of freedom
in this strange underworld that he could not find above ground. Bishop explored

parts of the cave far beyond his tour routes, discovering features that would be named Mammoth Dome, Bottomless Pit, and Cleveland Avenue. Because the cave is protected from the ravages of weathering, you can still see his name etched in the rock, looking as if he'd carved it last week.

Although not as celebrated as Bishop, other slave guides worked in Mammoth Cave as well— among them, Mat Bransford. In a twist of fate that folds with the pages of American history, Bransford's great-great-grandson, Jerry Bransford, proudly wears the National Park Service uniform as a tour guide.

Sometimes visitors on a tour will see cavers with headlamps and hardhats emerge from an adjoining corridor. They are either folks coming off the Wild Cave Tour or members of the Cave Research Foundation. Back in the mid 1990s I joined them to produce a television feature on the organization's ongoing efforts to map and explore new passageways. Donning hardhats, coveralls, headlamps, and kneepads, we headed into the remote regions of this mysterious subterranean world.

I wasn't really nervous about being down there. I grew up in a neighboring county, and as boys we frequently stooped or crawled through small openings in the earth searching for the next link to Mammoth Cave, much to the chagrin of our parents, if they were even aware. They remembered hearing stories from their own parents about the fate of legendary cave explorer Floyd Collins. In 1925 he too was searching for the next entrance to Mammoth Cave, but his foot got

Cave explorer Floyd Collins

On the ceiling of a Mammoth Cave passageway, gypsum formations look like flowers. In the days before the National Park Service took over management of the cave, "gypsum flowers" were often looted for souvenir sales.

wedged beneath a rock and he couldn't pull free. Despite the monumental efforts of rescuers to save him, he finally died of exposure after 14 days. It was a major world news event broadcast on the still new medium of radio. The old-timers of south central Kentucky never forgot it. An elderly friend of my family once said to me after hearing of my caving exploits, "Son, I learned something from Floyd Collins and that's to stay out of a damned hole."

Years later I was deep in Mammoth Cave, among scientists and expert cavers. The small team of explorers was either impressed with my backbreaking efforts to lug heavy camera gear down there or felt sorry for me. Either way, they allowed me to be the first to enter an unexplored room. There aren't many places left on earth that haven't been marked by humankind. This particular area was not laden with beautiful formations, and it lacked the grandeur of the gigantic rooms in the known cave, but the fact that I set foot where no human had ever been before was inconceivable to me. Perhaps in a small way I now had a sense of what early Native Americans and pioneer explorers like Walker, Boone, and Lewis and Clark must have felt as they gazed out upon places untouched by civilization.

The White Rocks of Cumberland Mountain. This mountain range was a barrier to settlers moving west.

CUMBERLAND GAP

Cumberland Gap National Historic Park is an awe-inspiring place that takes in more than 24,000 acres of mountainous terrain and 85 miles of hiking trails. Its focal point is Cumberland Gap itself, site of the Wilderness Road, one of the most important passageways in American history.

The Cumberland Mountain range rose above westward pioneers like a foreboding giant, unbroken and all but impenetrable until they came to a natural break where Tennessee, Virginia, and Kentucky meet. Beginning in the late 18th century, tens of thousands of settlers, eager to find a new life in the West, crossed into Kentucky at this critical point. It is believed that as many as 47 million people are descendants of these migrants who came through Cumberland Gap.

The top of the Pinnacle Overlook is a great place to reflect upon the significance of what took place at the Gap. I try to imagine the exhausted voyagers walking, sometimes barefoot, alongside their wagons and horses, hopeful but wary of entering "Kaintuck," a land the Native Americans called the "dark and bloody ground." I can only admire the tenacity it took to make this dangerous journey, but I also think of the disparity the Native Americans must have felt as they witnessed this relentless tide of European humanity pouring into their ancestral hunting grounds.

Down below in the Gap, I can almost hear the ghosts of these wayfarers who followed in the footsteps of Walker and Boone to a new beginning in the vast, unknown West. I can't comprehend what it must have been like to look out upon thousands of miles of wilderness, where we now see towns and highways.

Morning fog defines the circular shape of a crater at Middlesboro.

THE MIDDLESBORO IMPACT

As they came to the top of the Gap, the settlers could see what must have been very strange to them—a large, flat, bowl-shaped valley, seemingly out of place in this mountainous terrain. Little did they know they were looking down into a meteor crater.

In the early 1960s geologists came to a conclusion that would gain the attention of the scientific world—and, of course, the residents of small-town Middlesboro. Aside from the unusual round depression, easily seen in satellite photographs, down in the basin they discovered shocked quartz. The molecular makeup of the quartz had been changed by enormous heat and pressure, a change that occurs in only two ways: as a result of a nuclear bomb or a meteorite. It couldn't have been a nuclear bomb three hundred million years ago. That's when scientists believe that a rock the size of a building slammed into the earth at supersonic speed, blasting a crater about three miles in diameter. The energy released in the blast would have been 5,000 times more powerful than the atomic bomb dropped on Hiroshima. If such an event happened today, no one would be safe within 50 miles of the impact site.

Whenever I travel to Middlesboro and Cumberland Gap, I am reminded of two stories, one of humans and our age-old struggle for survival and a better life, and one of the cosmos and the awesome power that can be unleashed upon our small planet.

A bull elk eyes a cow at the Elk and Bison Prairie located in the Land Between the Lakes National Recreation Area.

THE RETURN OF THE BEASTS

In the late 1700s Daniel Boone could have heard a distant bull elk's bugle in the wilderness of "Kaintuck." He might have seen a herd of bison grazing across a field of prairie grass.

Two hundred years later, scientists at the Land Between the Lakes National Recreation Area (LBL) discovered a remnant patch of prairie grass, which confirmed their belief that the Great Plains ecosystem extended into western Kentucky and Tennessee.

Elk and bison were hunted out in Kentucky by the early 1800s, but this late 20th-century discovery encouraged wildlife biologists at LBL to attempt a restoration of native prairie grasses, and with it, a controlled reintroduction of the animals themselves. The plan worked.

In 1995, a 700-acre tract of forest and prairie was enclosed to contain herds of elk and bison for all to see. It is one of the places I go back to each time I visit the lakes and LBL. You can drive along a 3.5-mile loop road within the enclosure and watch these creatures in all their grandeur. Gaze out across the fields and watch bison slowly feeding on succulent grasses. Watch for the elk, and listen for the call of the bull—and imagine yourself back in time, before the European expansion into the new world and before the extirpation of these great beasts.

Hundreds of miles to the east, elk are thriving on the reclaimed strip mines and forests of eastern Kentucky. In fact, Kentucky boasts the largest wild elk herd east of the Mississippi, at more than 12,000 strong, all in 16 eastern Kentucky counties. This reintroduction began in 1997 when the Kentucky Department of Fish and Wildlife Resources released seven elk from western Kansas. No one could have imagined how successful this project would be. With funding provided by the

An early morning silhouette of a bull elk at a reclaimed strip mine in eastern Kentucky.

Rocky Mountain Elk Foundation, the Kentucky Department of Fish and Wildlife continued to release elk for several years. The survival rate, at 92%, was better than expected, and they are big. Eastern Kentucky's elk, which are now game animals because of the successful population growth, are on average 15% bigger than elk in the western United States.

THE BEAR PROJECT

Along with the elk, it is becoming more and more common to see black bears roaming the highlands. Bears roamed Kentucky long before we did, and they are coming back as a result of a decades-long natural migration from the mountainous states east of Kentucky. These days when I'm hiking in heavy bear country, I'll hike with another person and/or my dogs, and we will make plenty of noise as we sing, whistle, talk, and bark our way through the forest. Doing that ensures that the bears hear us in plenty of time to run away from this intimidating situation. Other hikers might run away too if they hear my singing.

Back in the early 1990s Kentucky wildlife biologists were still coming to grips with the relatively new black bear migration back into Kentucky. As host and producer of the Department of Fish and Wildlife's "Kentucky Afield," I came up with the idea of a television episode that would educate the public through our black bear biologist, Larry Short. But at that time it was still difficult to capture bear footage in eastern Kentucky. So we decided to head to Smoky Mountains National Park where bears are easier to find.

Larry Short and his assistant, Herbie Adams, joined a television crew and me on the trek to the Smokies. Park rangers told us that bears had been seen frequently at the base of Mount LeConte. So we headed into the wilderness with high hopes. As we hiked into some of the wildest country in the eastern United States, Larry told us about problems with bear and human encounters. "A lot of people tend to forget these are wild animals," he said. "They appear docile and cumbersome, to the point of being cuddly. Folks want to get close to the bears, pet them and feed them. This is inviting disaster. They have incredibly fast reflexes and can sprint up to 35 miles per hour."

Ursus americanus, the black bear. During the last 20 years, bears have been moving back into Kentucky from states east, primarily North Carolina.

Later a Park Ranger would tell us about a tourist who attempted to set his young child on the back of an adult black bear for a photograph. Fortunately, the bear chose to bolt instead of attack. But it could have been a tragedy.

"The few bear attacks that occur are usually unintentionally instigated by humans," Larry told us. If people would respect their space by staying back a considerable distance and never offer them food, bear attacks would be even more infrequent. And people who live in black bear country should keep household garbage in containers with lids and consider putting electric fences around gardens and bee hives. These measures would greatly reduce bear problems," he said.

A day and a half of hiking along the lower slopes of Mount LeConte had turned up nothing when finally, Larry spotted the first bear sign: claw marks on a tree. A few yards away, Larry found a decaying fallen tree that had been ripped open within the last couple of days. A bear had torn it apart looking for grubs. Then we nearly stepped in fresh bear scat. We now knew a bear was close at hand, and there was a good chance *Ursus americanus* was watching our every move.

"I can tell you boys are getting uneasy," Larry whispered. "I'd rather you have that attitude than try to go up and pet one," Herbie said with a grin. "Just remember, keep your distance as much as possible," Larry instructed. "I know you boys want to get good footage, but if you do get those cameras too close, the bear may run off or do just the opposite and charge. If he does come at you, there's a good chance it will be a bluff charge." (Black bears are noted for bluff charging—running at full force at a threatening presence, then coming to a grinding halt, sometimes just inches away from the unwelcome human.)

"You gotta just stand your ground," Larry told us. "You mean I gotta stand there while a bear comes at me at full force?" I asked. "That's right," Larry replied. "You sure as hell can't outrun them and they're great tree climbers, so going up a tree won't do you any good. If you stand your ground they're more than likely gonna bluff and then back off. Then all you have to deal with is a pair of wet trousers."

"How can folks avoid getting into that situation?" I asked. "It's just like we talked about before," Larry replied. "Don't purposely get too close and make a bear feel backed against a wall, so to speak. On the other hand, sometimes people can walk up on a bear if it's a windy day. Bears want to keep their distance from humans, unless they're used to being fed. But sometimes wind can prevent a bear from detecting the presence of humans through hearing and smell. To avoid that possibility, hikers should talk to one another and not try to sneak through the woods. Lone hikers might even consider singing to themselves, whistling, or possibly wearing bells on their backpacks."

Suddenly, with our eyes straining, we saw a black spot some distance away ambling through dense undergrowth. This was the moment we had been anxiously awaiting. We moved in somewhat closer, but not too close, for videotaping purposes. "It's a sow with two cubs," Herbie whispered. At this point our hearts were pounding with excitement. We began rolling our cameras, taking advantage of powerful zoom lenses. For an hour or so, the bear never acknowledged our presence. Perhaps she knew we were there, but we weren't close enough to intimidate her.

As is the case with most young creatures, people included, the cubs were full of energy, boundless energy. They climbed trees, swam in a nearby stream, and bounced and rolled around the sow, never giving her a minute's peace. Once she tried to lie down, but the cubs saw it as a golden opportunity to playfully maul her. She didn't try to stop them. It was as if she was just too tired to do much about it. It reminded me of our own mothers and just how much they give of themselves every day.

For this brief moment, everything was right. The bears were at peace in a wilderness of tall oaks, hemlocks, and pristine mountain streams. We rolled tape for the better part of an hour until the sow hurried her cubs up the mountain and out of sight. That was the last we saw of them.

THE GREAT DEER ATTACK

I've never had a bad encounter with a black bear, but I have with a whitetail deer. In the fall of 1989, I was producing a deer behavior television segment for my former employer, the Kentucky Department of Fish and Wildlife Resources. Bambi, as he was called, was a nine-point buck deer that lived in an enclosure at the department's game farm in Frankfort. Wildlife biologist Lauren Schaaf joined us in the enclosure to talk about the changes that occur in wild deer during the rutting season.

The first few minutes went fine. Lauren was a man of seemingly endless knowledge when it came to whitetail deer. He told me about buck deer and the swelling of their necks in the fall, making them stronger. "They have mood swings, too, and more of a willingness to fight other bucks—all signs of the breeding season," he said.

Lauren had just changed the subject to buck deer velvet, the hair-like substance that aids in the annual growth of a buck's antlers, when it dawned on me that Bambi had been circling us for quite some time. With each completed circle he seemed to get a little closer.

"What's that deer up to? He isn't going to charge us is he?" I asked. "Who knows what he's up to," Lauren replied. "He's probably got other things on his mind besides eating."

That lack of confidence in Lauren's response sent me an ominous signal—and for good reason. Bambi proceeded to lower his head and charge me with all the ferocity an enraged animal can muster.

Meanwhile, videographer Clint Goins was getting all this on camera, doing what a good videographer is supposed to do, I guess, while the rest of us fought for our lives.

Some 130 people nationwide are killed each year in deer/vehicle collisions, which makes deer the deadliest animal threat to human life in the United States. In this fuzzy picture taken from video, the author is getting rammed by a nine-point buck deer.

Bambi had now taken on three of us: Lauren, Johnny Widener, and me. Johnny was a Department of Fish and Wildlife employee who had seen the incident unfold and was attempting to rescue us. While Lauren tried to flip the deer over by grabbing his back legs and pushing on his rump, Johnny and I were in a more precarious situation up front—basically dangling on his antlers. Both of us were running out of strength.

Finally, we had to let go. As soon as we did, Bambi charged me again. I took a pretty good blow to the mid-section, but not bad enough to put me down. Then the enraged buck turned from me and charged Johnny, plowing him into the chain link fence of the enclosure. An antler had penetrated Johnny's leg. The situation was about to become critical when two more Fish and Wildlife employees rushed to the fence from the other side and managed to tie Bambi's antlers to the fence with a piece of rope.

The fight, which lasted nearly 45 minutes, was finally over. Lauren came out of it unscathed. Johnny suffered cuts, bruises, and a nasty leg wound that required minor surgery. Clint Goins got most of the incident on tape (which I will always be grateful for) until he too rushed in to help. For the next several days, I felt like I had been hit by an 18-wheeler. Bambi emerged from the fight uninjured, victorious, and meaner than ever.

The great deer attack aired on "Kentucky Afield" in October 1989 and became one of the most popular episodes in the show's long history.

THE ARCHES OF RED RIVER GORGE

Looking up from a low point on the trail, I watched other hikers make their way up a hillside littered with boulders the size of trucks. By the time they had climbed still higher to spectacular Gray's Arch, they looked as tiny as ants. Gray's Arch is just one of well over one hundred arches in the Red River Gorge Geological Area. With the highest concentration of natural sandstone arches in the eastern United States, Red River Gorge has been described as "Arches National Park with trees."

Managed by the US Forest Service and spanning 29,000 acres in Menifee, Powell, and Wolf counties, Red River Gorge has multiple designations—as a National Geological Area, a National Archaeological Area, a National Natural Landmark—and the Red River, which carved out the gorge, is itself a National Wild and Scenic River. The river, rusty red from natural iron deposits, meanders through the bottom of the gorge alongside a two-lane road with its own designation as a National Scenic Byway. There's even another designation. Of the 29,000 acres, 13,000 are known as the Clifty Wilderness, a federally designated Wilderness Area. This is the most rugged and primitive part of the Red River Gorge.

There are geological wonders everywhere you turn in the gorge—cliffs so tall and massive that rock climbers travel here from all over the world to take them on—and there are the arches, one after another, with names like Half Moon Arch, Double Arch, Rock Bridge, and Sky Bridge.

The process that formed these arches can take hundreds of thousands of years. Rain and melting snow flow down through tiny cracks in a sandstone ridge. Over time, the water widens the cracks, creating multiple ridges. The tops of the ridges are somewhat resistant to erosion, but water and wind are eating away the softer undersides.

Sandstone patterns at Red River Gorge look as though they were painted by an artist

Eventually the underside of one of the ridgetops will become so thin it will collapse, but the harder capstone will remain intact—hence, the birth of an arch. The arch itself will collapse someday, but new ones are being created every day. A cavity no bigger than a grapefruit could one day become a magnificent arch.

I did some math and figured that if you visited Red River Gorge once every season (four times a year) and hiked to a different arch each time, it would take you more than 25 years to see all the arches. I still have about 19 years to go. It's incredible that we have such a place in Kentucky that will keep us busy seeing new things well into our post-knee-replacement years.

◀ *Spectacular Gray's Arch at Red River Gorge National Geological Area.*

KENTUCKY'S LONG-DISTANCE FLIERS

Adjacent to Red River Gorge is Natural Bridge State Resort Park, with its own spectacular geological features. It was there that I learned about a study that would take me in a different direction from the rocks, arches, and overhangs. The project involved songbirds called "neo-tropical migrants"—dozens of species that spend their winters thousands of miles away in Central and South America and fly back to their North American breeding grounds in the spring.

Neo-tropical migrants include colorful birds like the bright red and black scarlet tanager and the beautiful indigo bunting, which ornithologists believe uses the stars to navigate from South America to its nesting site in the US. They travel these distances for the food sources available in our neck of the woods during breeding season—food sources that may not be available during the summer months in Central or South America.

Biologist Zeb Weese, formerly of the Kentucky State Nature Preserves Commission, led a nine-year study in the forest of Natural Bridge State Resort Park to learn more about these long-distance fliers. In the forest he set up nets so thin that we humans would not see them if we didn't know they were there. He checked them several times a day for unsuspecting songbirds that had flown into them. Zeb then safely removed the birds, recorded information such as species identification, gender, and approximate age, and banded the birds if they didn't already have a band from years past. From this study and others like it, scientists want to know how habitat losses on both ends of the journey are affecting populations.

◄ *The concentration on the face of biologist Zeb Weese is apparent as he delicately removes a neo-tropical migrant from a net.*

A neo-tropical migrant songbird is ready for release at Natural Bridge State Park.

I joined Zeb for a day in this dense forest to participate in the study and, hopefully, to see a neo-tropical migrant up close. As we made our way from one empty net to the next, I made sure I stayed behind Zeb out of fear I might walk right into a net without seeing it. Then, just as I had hoped, Zeb spotted a neo-tropical migrant—a hooded warbler caught in one of the nets. Within minutes, intense concentration showed in his face as he ever so delicately removed the bird from the net to prevent injury. Zeb then gently banded the bird with a pair of needle-nose pliers, opened his hand, and let the bird fly into the forest, quickly disappearing from sight.

I wished him a safe journey, as if you can say that to a little bird. But his mysterious ability to cross the heavens and know exactly where he is going is astounding to me.

BIG SOUTH FORK

To the south of Natural Bridge is another geological wonderland. Big South Fork National River and Recreation Area is characterized by weathered sandstone cliffs, overhangs, and arches. Encompassing 125,000 acres in Kentucky and Tennessee, you can visit here time and time again and never do the same thing twice. The area is managed by the National Park Service, but it differs from a national park because of its designation as a "recreation area," making it user-friendly for a wide array of outdoor activities, including hunting, which is rare in the National Park system. Here the National Park Service has found the middle ground between preservation and human access—and it has something for everyone, from backcountry campers to white water paddlers.

The central attraction is the Big South Fork of the Cumberland River, which flows through a deep gorge of sandstone walls and steep slopes—like a smaller version of the Grand Canyon and Colorado River. The scenery is spectacular, whether gazing up at the cliffs from river level, or looking down from the overlooks at the rim of the gorge.

The Big South Fork River has some class IV rapids at Angel Falls, more suited for expert paddlers, but much of the waters here are suited for beginning- to intermediate-level paddlers. I'll never forget my rafting experience with bouncing off house-sized boulders as we shot through a narrow called Devil's Jump—not quite as wild as Angel Falls, but thrilling nonetheless.

The park's natural arches alone provide plenty of material for photographers. Arches are found throughout the park, such as Twin Arches, a bizarre feat of nature as two arches, very similar in size, shape, and overall appearance, stand end-to-end.

One hundred fifty miles of trails take hikers and mountain bikers through this amazing country that includes dense forest, high vistas, and waterfalls such as Yahoo Falls, Kentucky's highest.

Horseback riders won't be outdone at Big South Fork. Riders can take on 180 miles of horse trails, the most of any National Park. Boarding and stabling facilities are available, but the only lodging in the park is the isolated Charit Creek Lodge, accessible only to horseback riders and hikers.

One of my most memorable experiences at Big South Fork began with a horseback ride to this rustic lodge. Guests stay in rooms without televisions and radios, which none of us on this trip missed. Meals eaten in candlelight and stories told around the table are fabulous. The meals are prepared by lodge managers (usually a married couple), who agree to live onsite for an extended period.

For those who do not relish this type of adventure, I recommend a train ride aboard The Big South Fork Scenic Railway, an open train with a tour guide aboard. Passengers board the train at Stearns, Kentucky, and ride into the park, where scenes of raw and stunning beauty abound in all directions.

Passengers on this scenic train ride come to the end of the line at Blue Heron, the name given a coal mining town established in 1937. Back then, the Stearns Coal and Lumber Company built this isolated community for a group of miners and their families working at mine 18. For them it was a life of grueling labor and occasionally fatal mining accidents. After mine 18 finally shut down in 1962, the community structures were either moved or fell into disrepair.

The Park Service re-created Blue Heron and mine 18 so visitors could see what life was like in an early 20th-century coal mining town. These days, a mining museum and open shells of buildings, known as "ghost structures," have push-button audio

◄ *Devil's Jump at The Big South Fork of the Cumberland River*

The restored coal tipple at the Blue Heron section of Big South Fork National River and Recreation Area.

recordings of the actual miners and their families recalling their hard existence. The coal tipple was reconstructed with a skywalk across the top, and the entrance to mine 18 was re-opened with historical displays.

Big South Fork is a land rich with human history, from Native Americans of thousands of years ago to 18th-century fur trappers—and recently the miners of the 20th century.

It is also a land of wild, rugged beauty, a magnificent example of the importance of the National Park Service and the lands it preserves for all of us and for generations to come.

LAND BETWEEN THE LAKES
AND THE TWIN LAKES

I've often said I think I could drive the Western Kentucky Parkway blindfolded. Over and over again, this is the road that has taken me to places like Kentucky Lake, Lake Barkley, and the Land Between the Lakes National Recreation Area.

Since I was a college student at Murray State University, I've frequented The Land Between the Lakes, commonly referred to as LBL. I like to drive up and down The Trace, a 45-mile north-south highway running through the middle of LBL. This scenic byway begins at Grand Rivers, Kentucky, and ends at Dover, Tennessee.

There are many side roads off The Trace. Every time I visit, I find one I've never seen before. These side roads lead to 300 miles of undeveloped shoreline along Kentucky Lake on one side and Lake Barkley on the other—two of the largest man-made lakes in the nation, with a combined 220,000 surface acres of water.

Walking along a shoreline and watching a glorious golden sunset is wonderful, but to me, to do it without any sign of human life is worth its weight in gold. This is one of the few places in the country where you can be on the waterfront for such a long distance and still find solitude.

For those who don't need the solitude, in LBL there are developed campgrounds and picnic areas, visitor centers with information and gifts, a planetarium for something a little different, and plenty of hiking and biking trails where you'll likely pass a human or two.

Meeting people is something I genuinely enjoy now that I have overcome the shyness and social awkwardness of my childhood. But I am a part-time loner, and

Kentucky Lake is beautiful in any season.
(Photograph courtesy of Tennessee State Parks)

LBL is a place where I can disappear. Aside from an occasional boat, I can see only wilderness and water for miles on end, and I can pretend there aren't so many of us on this little Earth.

✦ ✦ ✦

Another lake on the Kentucky/Tennessee border is worthy of writing about because it was created not by the hands of man, as were Kentucky and Barkley lakes, but by a cataclysmic natural event.

In the early 19th century all hell broke loose in the Mississippi River region of Kentucky, Tennessee, Arkansas, and Missouri. The land heaved, rolled, and shifted so violently that trees snapped like twigs as they were thrown back and forth. Hundreds of

Reelfoot Lake, created when a 25,000-acre chunk of land sank
in the Great New Madrid Earthquakes of 1811 and 1812.

earthquakes with three main shocks occurred between December 1811 and February 1812. They were among the strongest in history, according to scientists. The first main shock occurred on December 16 at 2:15 a.m., near what is now Blytheville, Arkansas. It had an estimated magnitude of 7.7. President Madison was awakened by the shaking in Washington, DC, 900 miles away. The second main shock, an estimated magnitude of 7.5, occurred on January 23. But the biggest quake was yet to come.

It happened at 3:00 a.m. near the Mississippi River town of New Madrid, Missouri (hence the name "The Great New Madrid Earthquakes"). Seismologists believe the shock may have reached a magnitude of 8.1. The earth split open, lifted, and sank, and the sandy soil along the Mississippi River shook until it turned into something like a milkshake, a phenomenon called liquefaction. Plaster fell off the

walls in Washington, DC, and church bells rang from the shaking in Charleston, South Carolina. Closer to the epicenter, settlers and Native Americans thought the world was certainly coming to an end this time. The Mississippi River raged from the stressing below, becoming an unbelievable scene of churning chaos, even appearing as if it were flowing backward. Nearby, a 25,000-acre chunk of land sank. The waters of the Mississippi flowed into it. From this hellish nightmare, Reelfoot Lake was born.

I remember learning about the San Andreas Fault and the Great San Francisco Earthquake of 1906 as a schoolboy, but not about the sleeping seismic giant in our own backyard. Memphis, St. Louis, and Paducah would sustain incredible damage if it happened with similar intensity today. The loss of life and temporary damage to the entire US economy could rival all natural disasters in American history.

Reelfoot Lake is a peaceful setting today. It is located primarily in Tennessee, with fingers extending north into Kentucky. But it looks like it belongs in Louisiana. Egrets flying above are so white they catch the farthest corner of your eye. Little mom-and-pop resorts with an air of the Deep South are tucked away in the bald cypress forest that lines the lakeshore. And speaking of cypress trees—some living examples can be found out in the middle of the lake. Theirs is an astonishing story of survival. They sank upright 200 years ago during the great quakes and still cling to life. Thousands of submerged cypress stumps across much of the bottom of the lake are the remains of trees that fell during the quakes.

The remaining stumps provide excellent habitat for bass, crappie, and hand-size bluegill. This place is an outdoor lover's dream. Nature photography is as good as it gets anywhere. White-tailed deer forage around the lakeshore, and bald eagles, egrets, and herons adorn the sky.

◀ *A fishing paradise born of a cataclysm. The bald cypress trees
and submerged stumps provide excellent habitat for crappie, bass,
and bluegill at Reelfoot Lake.*

Cypress trees live an average of 600 years, but it is believed
some have survived for 1,200 years.

I like to rent a small boat and take in the scenery in all its glory. But every time I go there, my imagination runs wild. This pristine, peaceful setting of fishermen and wildlife is actually a seismic zone with the potential to put all other earthquakes in the lower 48 to shame. Scientists say it is likely to happen again. Once again the song of a far-away calamity will ring the bells of Charleston. Anyone unfortunate enough to be on or near Reelfoot when it happens might just be swallowed up in the liquefaction or caught in the raging torrent the lake could become. I shouldn't make it sound so scary because it may not happen again for 100,000 thousand years. But I admit that this is one place where I don't doze off when the fish aren't biting.

BOOTS ON THE GROUND

If the last great wild places are worth saving, the Kentucky State Nature Preserves Commission (KSNPC) is on the front lines. Their employees are out there with boots on the ground, quietly walking through the hills, hollows, and wetlands of Kentucky, with trained eyes and dedication. The Commission inventories, monitors, and manages the rare, endangered, and threatened plant and animal species of our biologically diverse state. The KSNPC attempts to purchase those habitats and turn them into state nature preserves.

Currently, the Commission is responsible for protecting 61 nature preserves statewide. Metropolis Lake State Nature Preserve in McCracken County is a good example of what this agency manages to accomplish with its limited funds. This 123-acre natural lake (now protected) is ringed with cypress and tupelo trees, making it resemble wetlands in Louisiana or Florida. Tropical-looking egrets fly overhead. Axe Lake Nature Preserve in Ballard County looks like it should be full of alligators. Because of its latitude and its nearly 400-mile span from east to west, Kentucky is one of the more naturally diverse states in the nation, with a mix of the flora and fauna found in all regions of the United States.

Joyce Bender, KSNPC branch manager for Nature Preserves and Natural Areas, says Kentucky is "one-stop shopping for any natural community you might be looking for, including mountain habitats, floodplains and wetlands, cave systems, prairies, rich forests, and river systems." Some great examples are the discoveries made in the upper Green River in south central Kentucky. The Green has been recognized as one of the most important rivers in North America because of its indigenous species found nowhere else in the world. The Green's bottlebrush crayfish can grow to one foot long, and it looks like a lobster you would find in the ocean.

The author's favorite, the Kentucky sunsets of summer

Sadly, we are losing these habitats at an alarming rate for a reason you might expect: various kinds of development, from highways to houses. Another big threat is the vast influx of invasive species like kudzu, honeysuckle, and winter creeper. They simply overwhelm native species and wildlife habitats.

The small staff at the KSNPC keeps trudging ahead, fighting a monumental battle to save the last of our truly wild places. Fortunately for outdoor enthusiasts, most of the nature preserves are open to the public from sunrise to sunset. Because of the agency's priority—the protection of rare species—you can't camp or build fires or even bring your dogs. But you can bring your camera and go home with some incredible pictures of these last remaining pristine areas. The nature preserves are some of my favorite places to hike because I just might see something I won't see anywhere else in the world—not to mention its spell-binding scenery.

KENTUCKY WILDLIFE

The author gets up close and personal with a nonvenomous snake in eastern Kentucky. The timber rattlesnake, copperhead, western cottonmouth, and western pygmy rattlesnake are the four venomous snakes that can be found in the Bluegrass State.

A tiny grasshopper finds refuge in a lily.

A butterfly working a central Kentucky field hunts for nectar on a wildflower that is appropriately named the butterfly weed.

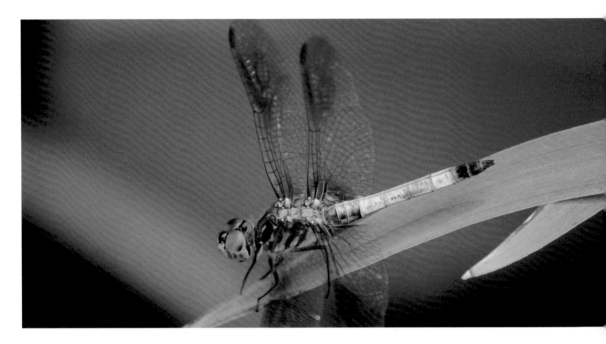

A dragonfly called the blue dasher poses for the author
near the banks of a farm pond.

An eastern box turtle on a Nelson County forest floor
exposes one of its red eyes, indicating he is a male.

A bull elk blends with native grasses at the Elk and Bison Prairie at the Land Between the Lakes National Recreation Area.

A doe and fawn are alerted to the author's presence on the shores of Kentucky Lake in Marshall County.

A giant swallowtail peers at the author's camera lens from behind a leaf in eastern Kentucky. With a wingspan that can reach up to six inches, the giant swallowtail is the largest butterfly in the United States.

"KENTUCKY SEASONS"

SPRING. *The author's son, Will, and Charlie wile away a spring afternoon in a field of daffodils (also known as March lilies).*

Perennial spring daffodils are all that remain of a 19th-century homesite in Taylor County.

A rare painted trillium brings spring to Black Mountain.

SUMMER. *Early morning sunlight shimmers through the fog of a Madison County forest.*

A lone boat makes its way across Dale Hollow Lake in late summer.

Windsurfer Austin Bates riding a summer breeze at Lake Barkley

FALL. An Anderson County forest turns golden in mid-October.

A mallard and his mirrored image on a Kentucky farm pond in late autumn

Autumn in the mountains of Bell County

Bright red and yellow maple leaves are caught in the fungus of a downed tree in Casey County.

A Kentucky sunset in late autumn.

Pumpkins are ripe for the picking at Boyds Orchard in Woodford County.

WINTER. *Winter on East Hickman Creek in Jessamine County.*

Although beautiful to look at, the ice storm of 2009 coated much of Kentucky, leaving more than half a million people without power for as long as weeks on end. The storm claimed more than a dozen lives.

Ice clings to everything, from power lines to twigs, in Kentucky's worst ice storm in modern history.

*Tina Edwards (left) and Eva Tucker (right) of Hopkins County carry on
the old Kentucky tradition of weaving baskets.*

THE HISTORY, PEOPLE AND CULTURE

◆ FINDING CHARLIE ◆

When I write about the history of Kentucky, I struggle with where to begin. Do I begin with the aboriginals who were here long before the Europeans? Do I start with Daniel Boone? No, for personal reasons I think I will begin in the Devonian geological period some 400 million years ago, when much of Kentucky was covered by a shallow sea. When I go seashell hunting I don't need to go to Sanibel Island, Florida. I can venture 10 minutes from my house in central Kentucky to one of my favorite road cuts and find plenty of shells, or at least the fossilized remains of them.

The beginning of my rock, mineral, and fossil collecting hobby (or obsession) began one summer afternoon about 2005. Bound for a story location, I was driving on a road near Taylorsville and realized I had made a wrong turn somewhere. Computer directions, cell phones, and navigation devices were technologies I had yet to come to grips with. I still struggled the old-fashioned way, by looking at road maps—and if that didn't work I would ask someone. That opportunity arose when I spotted a fellow on the side of the road. I slowed down and stopped across the highway from him, but I was a bit hesitant to get out of the car as I watched this rough-looking character with long, white, shoulder-length hair. His dirty white T-shirt and jeans looked like they hadn't seen a washer in a mighty long time—and the five-gallon bucket he was closely guarding surely contained all of his earthly belongings. I remember thinking, "Wait a minute. Maybe I should just drive away in case I'm walking into trouble here."

Then I thought of my friends and kinfolk in south central Kentucky. There were many days when we (myself included) sported our own dirty white T-shirts and

Charlie Oldham displays a few of his fossils and minerals.

jeans—and in our case, we added camouflage hats to the mix. So I got out of the car, crossed the highway, and approached the man. "How're you doing, sir?" I asked. "I'm a little lost and was wondering if you could point me in the right direction." "Maybe I can," he replied. Before he had a chance to give me directions, I asked him what the hammer in his bucket was for. "It's a rock hammer," he said. "I'm a geologist."

I nearly fell over, and I secretly kicked myself for "profiling." He introduced himself as Charlie Oldham, and he was, ironically, from Oldham County. He showed me some things he had found—bizarre-looking ancient sea creatures he called brachiopods, cephalopods, crinoids, and gastropods. Some were 400 million years old. The dinosaurs didn't exist yet when these animals were alive. (The vastness of geologic time is incomprehensible to me.)

As our conversation continued, Charlie told me that over the last half-billion years, this road cut has been under seas multiple times, and in future eons the place humans once called Kentucky will be under water again.

When highway construction crews blast through a hill, the strata are exposed. As you drive by these walls of sedimentary rock at 60 miles per hour, it's impossible to see the fossils revealed by the road cut. But central Kentucky, northern Kentucky, and the Cincinnati area are some of the best places in the country to find the fossilized remains of long-extinct marine life—and the Falls of the Ohio State Park in southern Indiana, right across the Ohio River from Louisville, is the best known example of a Devonian fossil bed in the United States. Park visitors are not allowed to pick those up. But there are several geological clubs in Kentucky that offer field trips to their members—to locations where you can take home specimens. This is how my fossil eye developed. I can now spot a highly sought-after trilobite, the predecessor of a horseshoe crab, from several feet away.

Years after that day on the side of the road, I still collect fossils and minerals with Charlie whenever I can. We've become rock-hounding friends—and I've learned more about his storied past. He's been a rock-hounder since he was what he calls a "pebble pup." By the time he was 14 he'd amassed a large collection of fossils and minerals. But for reasons he still doesn't understand, his father didn't approve of his hobby. One day he gathered Charlie's entire collection and threw it away. It was a shortsighted act that was devastating to Charlie, but it made him even more determined to pursue his passion for rock collecting.

The only time he stopped collecting was during his tour in Vietnam. After surviving being shot down in a helicopter, Charlie returned home to Kentucky and decided to make a career out of his passion for rocks. He went to college on the G.I. Bill and became a geologist for Kentucky state government.

Charlie is retired now, but he still gets out, poking around road cuts or any other place he thinks has the potential to hold great specimens. His long, white hair is still in a ponytail and his clothing is as unkempt as ever.

Charlie has given me priceless knowledge of geology that I have tried to pass on to my own daughter and son. My daughter, Miranda, now an adult, says she can't wait to go with me on my next geode hunting trip—her own hobby being a result of my finding a new friend on the side of a lonely Kentucky highway.

Thirteen thousand years ago seems like last weekend compared to the geologic time periods Charlie and I look back on. But as for human existence in what is now the United States, that's a very long time ago. And it is approximately the length of time archaeologists believe nomadic hunters and agrarian peoples lived in what we know as Kentucky.

Once I followed a team of archaeologists into the deep woods of the Daniel Boone National Forest to an ancient campsite under a rock overhang. I watched these scientists delicately peel back the layers of soil as if they were turning back the pages of an ancient history book. Blackened soil from fires, bits of pottery, and other evidence turned up in layers—one society a few inches under the other, representing thousands of years of occupation of this one rock house.

Hunting for Native American artifacts is a pastime I dearly love. I don't look for them in places where it's not allowed, such as rock overhangs, burial grounds, or public land, but in privately owned crop fields right after they've been plowed in the spring—and only if I have permission from the landowner. A plowed field on high ground near a water source is potentially a great place to look for flint and stone tools used thousands of years ago for hunting and gathering purposes. And even though some fields may have been picked over for decades, they will sometimes continue to produce artifacts. How could this be possible? When I think of modern Americans and how much we have dropped or thrown on the ground just over the last 250 years, it makes sense to me why so much evidence can be found of Native Americans who were here for at least 13,000 years.

Contact with the Europeans was the beginning of the end of aboriginal dominance in North America. The Europeans would come in unrelenting numbers, and the native people would ultimately be pushed out of the way.

At the 150th anniversary of the Battle of Perryville, hundreds of Confederate re-enactors charge up a hill. The real battle took place on October 8, 1862. It was the largest battle in Kentucky, and a bloody one, with nearly 8,000 casualties in one day.

That has been the way of our human existence: one culture pushing another out of the way over land and resources. The Native Americans themselves were known to do this as well. The land that is modern-day Kentucky was called the "dark and bloody ground" because various tribes fought one another to claim its resources and abundant game.

In 1775 frontiersman Daniel Boone blazed his Wilderness Road through the Cumberland Gap and into Kentucky, founding the early western settlement of Boonesborough. Boone's exploits and popularity helped to stir the restless souls who longed for a new beginning. At least 200,000 settlers made the perilous journey through the gap and into the unknown.

◆ BACKWOODS FIGHTERS ◆

By the time of the American Revolution, a fledgling Kentucky militia was put to the test, not always by the British themselves, but also by mercenaries hired by the British. Kentucky's most famous battle of the Revolution took place at the Blue Licks salt flats in what is now Robertson County. On August 19, 1782, trailblazer Daniel Boone, now one of the commanders of 182 militiamen, feared he might be walking right into an ambush after noticing a suspicious-looking sign. But other officers were anxious to make a daring march forward in pursuit of British and Indian forces who were trying to drive the settlers out of the Kentucky territory. Boone was right. The American troops were ambushed and suddenly found themselves in brutal hand-to-hand combat. In a resounding defeat, 72 Kentuckians were killed, including Daniel Boone's son Israel. Only seven of the 300 British/Indian fighters were killed. The Battle of Blue Licks would go down in history as the last battle of the American Revolution and an American defeat.

Although it was a war that all too few know about today, the War of 1812 would place Kentucky's militiamen on a much higher plane. Once again they faced the British

*Union re-enactors portray officers in the 13th
Kentucky Regiment of Infantry Volunteers.*

*A re-enactor plays the music of the Civil War era
at the 150 anniversary of the Battle of Perryville.*

and their Indian allies in the war that is often referred to as "the second American
Revolution." Kentucky supplied most of the troops (25,000) in the war effort and, as a
result, suffered more casualties than all other states. At least 1,200 were killed in such
battles as the Battle of River Raisin, in which 400 Kentuckians lost their lives. The
Kentucky boys would earn a reputation as a tough bunch of backwoodsmen.

Our backwoods ruggedness and willingness to fight would not be lost in the
generations that followed. Kentucky supplied more than 100,000 men to the
Union or Confederate cause during the Civil War. The 13th Kentucky Regiment
of Infantry Volunteers is a good example of the strength and spirit of the
Kentuckians. This Union outfit, consisting primarily of country boys from south

Union re-enactors portray the ferocious, bloody encounter that was the Battle of Perryville.
Although it was a tactical victory for the Confederates, the number of Union reinforcements
in the area halted any plans for a continued Confederate advance into Kentucky.

central Kentucky, fought in one battle after another across the western theater, including the Battle of Shiloh.

In his memoirs, Regiment Captain Elijah Tucker wrote, "I saw many hardships and endured much exposure and my life was almost continuously in danger, yet I look back to the three years and four months I spent in the Army as among the happiest years of my life."[1] In this "great adventure," half of the regiment's soldiers did not come home. Many were killed outright on the battlefields. Others died from battle wounds that wouldn't heal, and many others died of disease and sickness.

---

1. "My Life Has Not Been a Blank: The Autobiography of Captain Elijah F. Tucker of Greensburg, Kentucky," by Bruce Curtis. Louisville, KY: *Filson Club History Quarterly 64* (April 1996) 264–276

My own great-great-grandfather, Michael Shuffett, was likely the last casualty of the 13th. He survived being wounded in action at the Battle of Resaca in Georgia, only to contract kidney disease from unsanitary camp conditions. He lived with the disease until 1872, when he died at his home in Green County at the age of 29.

✦ AGELESS LERA WILLIAMS ✦

In the grand scheme of things it hasn't been that long since the country was torn apart by the Civil War. In Campbellsville, Lera Williams told me about her father's vivid memories as a young boy of General John Hunt Morgan's raiders, storming through southern Kentucky. Alexander Morrison was born in 1856. His daughter lived until 2011. Therefore, only one generation separated the Civil War from the technological age of the 21st century.

Lera Williams was born February 1, 1900, and lived to the age of 111. When I interviewed her for a story she was 110, the oldest living Kentuckian and the 16th oldest living person in America.

I didn't know what to expect as I made my way along an old cracked sidewalk toward the little house on Meader Street in Campbellsville. I was about to meet someone who was already considered a senior citizen when I was born in 1958. But how would she handle the lights and cameras? Was her mind still sharp? Would she be able to hear my questions?

Upon knocking on the door, an elderly gentleman, one of Lera Williams' children, invited me in. There they were, Lera and her six surviving children, including her 91-year-old daughter, Eloise, who moved around the room like someone 30 years younger.

"Hello, everybody, and it's an honor to meet you, Ms. Lera." She looked up at me from her favorite chair and said, "Nice to meet you, too, and I'm doing fine and dandy." Her mind was still sharp, all right. In fact, it was hard to match her wit. "I think we'll look real cute together on TV," she said with a bright and ageless smile. The whole room broke out in laughter, and I was reminded that "Mama is quite the flirt."

In 1918, Lera married lifelong farmer C.M. Williams, who died of cancer in 1961. She had been a widow longer than she was married, living so long that when I met her she was known as a "supercentenarian," a person 110 years of age or older.

As I interviewed her, I asked, "How do you feel about becoming such a star?" "I'm just thrilled to death. Why, I never thought it could happen to little old me," she said with a big smile. "That's right, little old me, a star!" she repeated. Again, the whole room broke out in laughter.

Of course I wanted to know her secret to longevity. She told me her secret was not to worry. "Don't worry, don't worry, don't worry. God is watching out for you," she pointed out. Then she sang me a few verses of an old song that had the same lines.

Deborah Danner, Ph.D., of the Sanders-Brown Center on Aging at the University of Kentucky, said that kind of attitude is common among centenarians. "They all seem to have this innate ability to let things roll off of them, no matter how many bad things have happened. To them, it's all good," she said.

Dr. Danner participated in the famous Nun Study on aging, Alzheimer's and other brain diseases, following more than 600 Roman Catholic Sisters of Notre Dame in Minnesota. The ongoing study, which began in 1986, looked into the reasons why so many nuns live to a ripe old age and included an examination of the writings of the nuns as far back as their teenage years. Dr. Danner said the findings were astonishing. The nuns who wrote about their lives in a positive way—the glass is half full—lived an average of nine years longer than the other nuns. Dr. Danner said less stress puts less stress on the vital organs.

When the author was born in 1958, supercentenarian Lera Williams
of Taylor County was already considered a senior citizen.

But Lera's life had not been without tragedy. On an unusually warm day in January 1929, the skies grew ominous in Taylor County. A supercell thunderstorm produced a strong tornado that demolished the Williamses' farmhouse. Their six-month-old daughter, Nellie Katherine, was killed. Later Lera lost another child, Audrey, to an illness. "How did you cope with that?" I asked. With an answer that goes right along with Dr. Danner's studies, Lera said, "You just gotta go on and do the best you can. That's all you can do."

But a positive outlook on life is not the only ingredient in a rare combination of mental and physical traits, according to the Sanders-Brown Center's director, Dr. Linda Van Eldik. "They have a rare combination of genetics (someone else in the family lived a long life), positive attitudes, healthier lifestyles (reasonably good eating habits), and just plain luck—no lethal accidents or cancers, etc."

Lera's children brought out a feast of country cooking on the day I visited. The table was adorned with pork loin, green beans and corn canned from the garden, homemade biscuits, and some of the best pecan pie I've ever eaten. When Lera finished her dinner (still the noontime meal in much of rural Kentucky), I asked her about her diet. She said she had always eaten a lot of fruit and vegetables, chicken, fish, and eggs, her favorite. "And right now I'd love to have some dry-roasted peanuts," she added, as she looked toward one of her daughters.

Ms. Lera was a classic example of how to live to a 100 or more. You have to laugh a lot, sing a lot, as Lera did for me, don't worry too much because "it won't do you any good," eat fairly well (lots of fruits and vegetables), and stay reasonably thin as Lera had. And it would help if you have someone in your immediate family who lived unusually long too: Lera's half-brother, John Morrison, lived to be 104 years and six months.

In my own unscientific study of centenarians (in television interviews), I've found that these folks always look forward to tomorrow. They don't dwell on the past and especially not the bad parts of their past. Life goes on. The sun will rise tomorrow. But that's hard for many of us. I doubt if I would ever get over losing a child in a tornado. Maybe they don't, either. But they definitely have the remarkable ability to at least put it aside and keep going. At the end of my wonderful day with Ms. Lera, she reminded me of "how cute we look together." On that note, I left the little house on Meader Street and vowed to at least try to learn from her. I will try to find solutions to problems without stressing out so much. I will look forward to the rising sun of a new day, no matter how many bad things happen to me today. Heck, I might even start singing more often, at least in the shower.

Country music star Wynonna Judd is enjoying her day aboard the Santa Train.

✦ THE SANTA TRAIN ✦

In my job, I have had the good fortune of meeting some amazing folks, from centenarians to celebrities. Often they impress me so much that I am left with everlasting memories of them. One such person was with me aboard the Santa Train.

The hours were as bad as Santa's on Christmas Eve. On a cold November morning in 2009, long before sunrise, I was barely awake and drinking all the coffee I could get my hands on in preparation for hosting a television segment.

Country music star Wynonna Judd was born Christina Claire Ciminella in Ashland, Kentucky, in 1964. She is the daughter of Naomi Judd and the half-sister of movie star Ashley Judd. Wynonna is a multiple Grammy Award winner and a *New York Times* best-selling author.

The Santa Train attracts a crowd of parents and children on the Kentucky/Virginia state line.

At 5:30 a.m. the CSX train I was aboard headed out for a 110-mile trip, loaded with 15 tons of toys and food to be given to children in Appalachia.

Country music star and Kentucky native Wynonna Judd was also on board at that painful hour. Clearly remembering her roots and ties to the mountains, Wynonna had volunteered to give away food and toys and to greet folks along the way. The efforts of not only Wynonna but other volunteers, donors, and the CSX Railroad Company demonstrated the true spirit of Christmas.

Our first stop was Shelby, Kentucky, at 6:30 a.m., then Marrowbone at 7:00 and Elkhorn City at 7:30, then on to such little towns in Virginia as Haysi, Dante, and Kermit and on to our final destination of Kingsport, Tennessee.

As I helped throw toys from the train while the camera rolled, I was touched to see the exuberance in the faces of the children. For some, these little things we tossed to their outstretched arms would be the nicest gifts they would receive this Christmas. In a down economy in an already distressed region, this was a grand event. On stops where we got off the train, I often handed out gifts alongside Wynonna. Her arms were always loaded down with gifts that she juggled while trying simultaneously to greet throngs of people. She said her motivation to work this hard came from a strong desire to give back to people who weren't as fortunate as she was.

She also worked pretty hard between stops aboard the train. At one point she mentioned that her hand was getting tired as she autographed and gave away dozens of CDs to the volunteers, media, and CSX staff.

I didn't know Wynonna Judd before that day, and I never dreamed I'd be handing out gifts with her. But I came to know and admire a superstar who hadn't forgotten where she came from—and was down-to-earth, humorous, and big-hearted. I believe those are the qualities that all the stars of the entertainment world should possess.

OUR STORIED TOWNS

⋄ NOBOB ⋄

Truths, half-truths, and folklore have given Kentucky a wealth of unusual place names, such as Bugtussle, Blackgnat, Monkey's Eyebrow, Egypt, Mistletoe, and Hell-fer-Certain. As I travel through these communities I'm left scratching my head and anxious to learn the story behind the names. One such place is the community of Nobob in Barren County.

There's not much left, if there ever was much in Nobob. I saw three or four houses with no one outside them and the abandoned Nobob post office, an old wooden building still standing, but wearily. The only sign of life around here was an old beagle mix lying beside the post office, yawning as if he too were bored with the nothingness of this place.

Probably the most exciting thing that ever happened in Nobob gave birth to the town's name. Legend has it that sometime in the late 18th century a fellow named Bob camped here with a party of hunters. For reasons unknown, Bob wandered away from camp alone one day and never returned. For days his friends searched for him, returning to camp each day with the pronouncement, "No Bob."

Bob's remains are likely still out there somewhere, in a farmer's field or a patch of woods, and you have to wonder what happened to him in the wilds of 18th-century Kentucky. His end may have been tragic, but his legacy has left generations of Nobobians (maybe six or seven people and at least one old dog) with a great story to tell about their community. Thanks, Bob.

Some of our communities have a past right out of the Old West, like Adairville in Logan County. When I visited this little town I learned there was trouble here as early as 1806, when Andrew Jackson fought a duel.

Jackson, a major general and a Tennessee lawyer, had a series of disputes with another lawyer named Charles Dickinson. The two argued and traded insults over a horse race involving Jackson's horse and a horse belonging to Dickinson's father-in-law. The rift got worse when Dickinson publicly criticized Jackson and his wife, Rachel, perpetuating the rumor that Rachel's first husband had never officially divorced her. As time passed, the antagonism between the two escalated to name-calling, with Dickinson calling Jackson a "worthless scoundrel" and Jackson saying to Dickinson, "You are a cowardly talebearer."

Finally, Jackson challenged Dickinson to a duel. Because duels were illegal in Tennessee, they met across the state line in Kentucky near Adairville. On May 30, 1806, they walked their paces until they were about 20 feet apart. When they turned around Dickinson fired his pistol first. Jackson didn't even flinch. According to the dueling rules of the day, Dickinson then had to stand and wait for Jackson to fire. Jackson took careful aim and shot Dickinson in the abdomen, fatally wounding him.

Jackson soon realized that he had been shot, too. Dickinson, known for his shooting skills, hit Jackson in the chest, very near his heart. Jackson survived, although the bullet, which was never removed, caused him pain for the remaining 39 years of his life. The course of American history could have been drastically altered had the outcome of the duel gone the other way. Andrew Jackson became the seventh President of the United States and, as we used to say back home, he was "a man who'd jist as soon kill ya as look atcha."

Decades later, an Adairville farmhouse became the hideout for a pair of notorious bank robbers. The home belonged to Jesse and Frank James's aunt and uncle, George

Historians disagree on how many duels Andrew Jackson fought. The estimates range from 10 to 100. But not all duels of the day ended with fatal shots, which is likely why Jackson lived through so many. Rivals often intentionally fired their pistols into the air or at a safe distance away from each other. Disputes ended with both parties living to brag to their grandkids about fighting a duel.

and Nancy Hite. When the law got a little too close out West, the brothers high-tailed it to their aunt and uncle's place in Kentucky, passing the time by planning more robberies—and carrying them out in nearby towns. Ironically, the James boys were the sons of a Baptist preacher, also a native Kentuckian.

Fellow gang member Bob Ford fatally shot Jesse in 1882. By then Jesse and Frank had become national celebrities and the subjects of dime-store novels.

The gunslingers of old Adairville are now the topics of tourism promotion. Time has healed this town. Now the community boasts an award-winning school system and a low crime rate. Folks around town have a Southern charm and are eager to promote their antique stores, mom-and-pop restaurants, and unique shops. They want you to "stay awhile or a lifetime." Just be glad you're visiting this town nowadays.

✦ SHELL-SHOCKED HAWESVILLE ✦

Before and during the Civil War, Hawesville, the county seat of Hancock County, was a wild, drinkin', gamblin' town. Even the town doctor, Hardin Davidson, was not a model citizen. The doctor shot and killed a fellow in 1859. He wasn't charged, but a few months later Doc Davidson detonated a bomb in an attempt to blow up another fellow. But it was the doctor himself who died from injuries sustained in the blast.

During the Civil War, Federal troops bombed Hawesville from across the Ohio River on the Indiana shore—and from

The Hite House near Adairville was a frequent hideout for outlaws Frank and Jesse James.
The old farmhouse is in need of restoration.

Union gunboats on the river— because Hawesville harbored marauding Confederate guerillas, including Doc Davidson's son, Captain William Davidson. The younger Davidson died from gunshot wounds in 1865 as he was burning down the Owensboro-Daviess County Courthouse. His death came just five years after his father got too close to a bomb he had set off.

Today, Hawesville is a peaceful, picturesque little river town with a lot to see, including the Hancock County Museum, which showcases steamboat art and replicas. Townspeople are friendly, and even the doctors around there are law-abiding citizens.

In his time Jesse James was looked upon by many people as somewhat of a folk hero, but he killed 16 people singlehandedly and is believed to have been involved in the murders of 150 others.

A two-lane road winds its way through the rolling countryside of Owen County and eventually into the heart of Sweet Owen, Kentucky, population, a handful. The community got its name from a comment made by Kentuckian John C. Breckinridge while running for US Congress in 1851. His opponent, ahead in the race, asked Breckinridge to concede. Breckinridge said, "No, I'm waiting for Sweet Owen (meaning Owen County) to come through for me." Well, the county did and Breckinridge won, barely. In honor of the victory, Owen County folks gave one of their communities the name "Sweet Owen."

In 1856 Breckinridge was elected US vice president, the youngest in history when he was inaugurated at the age of 36. He lost a presidential bid in 1860, and, at the outbreak of the Civil War, the now bitter Breckinridge switched sides, becoming a major general and commander of the famous Kentucky Orphan Brigade of the Confederacy.

There are only a few people living in Sweet Owen. You'll find the main hub of activity at the Sweet Owen general store, where you can buy groceries, hardware, guns …and tell some tall tales. The little town that's no more than a dot in the road has a claim to fame from a statement made by a man who would become a vice president of the United States and a Confederate commander. It's amazing what's in a name.

The lights of downtown Louisville as seen from across the Ohio River in Indiana.
Revolutionary War General George Rogers Clark founded Louisville in 1778,
naming it after King Louis XVI of France.

The story of Paducah is told in murals on its Ohio River floodwall. The murals, painted by artist Robert Dafford, are three city blocks long. Paducah was founded in 1827 by William Clark, younger brother of General George Rogers Clark, who founded Louisville.

◆ WHEN HELL CAME FROM THE HEAVENS ◆

When people ask me where I'm from, I often tell them, "a Norman Rockwell painting." My roots run deep in the little historical town of Greensburg, the county seat of Green County, in south central Kentucky. I see myself as lucky to have been raised in an environment where everyone knows everyone as well as everything about everyone. As uncomfortable as that may seem, it mostly comes from a sense of caring for one another. In the old time postcard that is my hometown, help was never far away in times of tragedy.

In September 2011, I was part of a crew producing television segments that featured small communities across the Commonwealth. This one was about a picturesque little town of 3,500, tucked away in the foothills of Appalachia. I remember writing the first few lines and thinking how the residents would appreciate some publicity as this community was off the beaten path.

The town I was writing about is one we've all heard of now: West Liberty. The peaceful little town that I loved, that reminded me so much of my own, was forever changed by one day in March 2012.

A "perfect storm" of colliding air masses was taking place overhead, and by the early morning hours of March 2, the National Weather Service was confident enough to give people a dire warning. Our region of the country, including all of Kentucky, would be ground zero for a likely outbreak of "strong, long-lived tornadoes." The prediction was accurate. By mid-afternoon tornadoes were tearing across southern Indiana, destroying little communities like Henryville. Later in the day, supercell thunderstorms had produced killer tornadoes in Boone, Kenton, Menifee, Pulaski, and Laurel counties in Kentucky. And just after 5:30 p.m. that day, hell came from the heavens over West Liberty, the county seat of Morgan County. As if directed by some evil force, a ferocious tornado severely damaged the local hospital just outside of town, dropped off Wells Hill (taking a forest with it), crossed the Licking River, then roared right toward the center of West Liberty. Those who saw it coming could not believe their eyes.

People of the Appalachians feel more protected than those living in flatlands. The hills and mountains usually act as something of a barrier against tornadoes, draining their strength or stopping them. But this nearly mile-wide monster entered West Liberty as an EF3 (enhanced Fugita scale) packing spinning winds of around 150 mph, and possibly higher at times. Sturdy brick and stone buildings were demolished, cars were tossed and mangled, houses were wiped off their foundations and government buildings were destroyed. Tragically, seven people were killed and hundreds injured or left homeless.

A car lies upside down amid the debris that was once a home in West Liberty.

We went back to the little town I had written about months before. This time our story was not a pleasant one. We were now at work on a special production about tornado recovery across the state. West Liberty would be the focal point.

The twister hit West Liberty exactly in the center of town, then plowed through another 36 miles of Morgan County, striking other small communities. In the aftermath, West Liberty was now unrecognizable to me. And I saw things impossible to understand. Dozens upon dozens of homes were simply gone, while other homes were lifted off their foundations and set down nearby, damaged but intact. A sign from downtown West Liberty reading "Seasons Florist" was found some 100 miles away in West Virginia—in the backyard of a retired florist. A horse was lifted from its field and deposited inside the roofless home of its owner, where it stood calm

A sign reading "Haven of Hope" survives the twister that destroyed downtown West Liberty.

in the kitchen, uninjured, incomprehensively surviving being airborne in the midst of flying metal, glass, brick, and wood. Throughout the incredible 90-mile track of this particular twister, bizarre scenes prevailed, like two heavy copper pipes found twisted into a braid so close to perfect that it would put a hairstylist to shame.

There are countless stories of sacrifice and courage. As the twister roared over Main Street in West Liberty, Morgan County Judge Executive Tim Conley looked out the glass door of the city municipal building and was horrified to see an elderly woman trying unsuccessfully to open it. The wind was forcing it shut. With nearly superhuman strength and adrenaline, the judge, with the help of Emergency Commander Mike Lacy standing behind him for support, pushed open the door against the incredible force of a twister and pulled the woman inside. Looking out the glass door one last time before the building began to explode, Judge Conley witnessed a scene that will stay with him for the rest of his life. He recalls, "Inside the vortex it was an eerie dark, brownish color. Everything imaginable was spinning and flying in the air, and cars were rolling and sliding up and down the street."

Back home in south central Kentucky, we have seen more than our fair share of tornadoes. A killer F4 hit Adair, Green, and Russell counties in the spring of 1971, killing six people along its track. Then, in what is known as the super outbreak of April 1974, I was a stunned 15-year-old watching live news coverage of a strong tornado tearing across Louisville when I decided to take a quick look out the window to see what the skies looked like at home. For a couple of seconds I couldn't believe what I was seeing. Maybe it was a barn on fire. But the column of smoke was moving! To my shock I realized I was watching a tornado near my house at the same time another one was hitting Louisville, about 90 miles away.

The aftermath of our county's second F4 in three years left me dumbfounded. Aside from hundreds of destroyed homes and barns, I saw a boat hanging in the power lines. Large boulders half buried in the ground along a creek were pulled out, and dead cattle were found in pastures other than their own.

From that day forward, I learned everything I could about tornadoes, from what's going on inside the thunderstorms that give them birth to the unbelievable power of an EF5 twister.

Three days after the storm I went to West Liberty. Amid the rubble, I looked down at my feet at a Border Collie, shaking nervously. As I knelt down to calm her, she ran off. There were hundreds of emergency personnel in town that day, and

The "super outbreak" of April 3 and 4, 1974, is known as the most violent outbreak of tornadoes in recorded history. Of the 148 tornadoes that touched down over those two days, an unusually large number of them were classified as F3 or more. At least six reached intensities of F5, which may have wind speeds that top 300 mph. The outbreak killed 330 people across six states, including Kentucky. The hardest hit community in Kentucky was the town of Brandenburg, where 31 people lost their lives.

I watched the dog run up to several of them, sniff at their feet, and run off again. She was obviously confused, maybe not even knowing where she was any more. Perhaps her home was destroyed and her master injured, or even worse. Her simple existence turned upside down, the little dog with black and white patches disappeared into the heaps of twisted rubble, the strange smells, and the deafening noise of chainsaws and dozers. I will always wonder what happened to that little dog.

As for the townsfolk, their best was brought out like never before. They helped each other in the days and weeks after the storm, and many became fatigued to the point of total exhaustion. It is what folks in these hills do. Their tenacious spirit will prevail. One man told me, "We will build it all back as fast as we can." New homes and buildings will once again line the streets.

Along with government agencies, people from all walks of life and all points across the country poured into West Liberty. Three months after the storm, more than 600,000 volunteer hours had been logged. Like Greensburg, Kansas, which was also destroyed by a twister, West Liberty will become another national model of how small towns can recover from the ill winds of a super-tornado. Someday normalcy will return to West Liberty. But the emotional scars will always be there, and no one in either West Liberty or the other communities devastated by the outbreak of March 2012 will ever forget the day hell came down from the heavens.

◆ THE SHOW MUST GO ON ◆

As a teenager, when I looked out the window and saw a tornado for the first time, I ran outside to get a better look, as grapefruit-size hailstones rained down all around me. I doubt if I'd be alive today if one of those things had hit me on the head. Going outside, unbeknownst at the time to my parents, was a terrible mistake in judgment. Throughout my life I have made many of these, so many mistakes that I cringe when I think back on them. But at least my career choice was not one.

My wealth comes from traveling down highways, byways, and dirt roads, seeking out positive stories of people and places. The stories are in my head—and they are scribbled on 10,000 unorganized pieces of paper. The pictures are stored away on memory sticks and disks, waiting to be looked upon in grander fashion. And new stories are being uncovered every day as the years roll on and I grow older. I plan to keep seeking out stories as long as I am blessed with good health, a broad-brimmed hat, a walking stick, and an old dog by my side.

◆ BEHIND THE SCENES ◆

The making of a television series is a task of variables. Normally there is a crew of talented people with me, but if bad weather or technical issues have delayed a field production, or it is a segment up against its deadline, and a crew isn't available, I'll "one-man-band" the piece. In other words, I'll act as the cameraman, the audio engineer, the lighting director, the host, and the producer all in one. It's a workout that strains mind and muscles.

At the time of the publication of this book, I've been a television host and writer for over 25 years. In traveling from one end of the state to the other, I've either been involved in or produced thousands of television features—and I've met just as many great people.

The most watched in-house production in KET's history was a show I had the honor of hosting called "Kentucky's Last Great Places." Using a book with the same title as a reference, we headed off to the most remote, pristine natural features our state has to offer. The main reason we still have these places is because they are nearly impossible, or at least very hard, to get to. Our mission was to bring awareness to the importance of protecting wild areas such as these and to give the viewers a chance at least to see them on television even if they couldn't get there.

The author's famous television co-host, Sadie, traveled with him for thousands of miles, back and forth across Kentucky.

With walking stick and canine co-host Sadie by my side, I was filmed hiking through dense forests, climbing up cliffs, crawling through caves, floating down rivers, and walking through prairies of head-high wildflowers. The crew, the dog, and I were put to the test physically, and by the end of the production we had racked up quite a large number of injuries. But we all felt proud to be a part of it.

"Last Great Places" will live in my memory for the rest of my life, but some of my fondest memories involved what we called "road show specials." We picked highways that cross Kentucky and traveled their entire length, showcasing people and places along the way. To date we've done highways 68, 60, and 62.

The author's television co-host Charlie was so well trained that he often patiently posed for photographers wearing a hat.

To the viewers at home, it looked like I took a leisurely trip down the road for a couple of days; just me and my dog, stopping along the way to visit interesting attractions, towns, and local folks. In reality, I had two vans behind me crammed full of gear and six or seven people. It takes more than just a couple of days to get a program like that finished in the field; a couple of months would be more accurate. We would go home to our families on the weekends, and then drive back to our last location on Sunday evenings, picking up where we left off.

The casual trip through town, stopping here and there for a few minutes, could take two days to shoot. We had to get dozens of community shots and interview local residents as well. That's why KET provided me with two sets of the same outfit.

By the end of a hot, humid, 12-hour day one, I could get up the next morning with a fresh set of clothes. I'm not sure whether this was done for my benefit or the benefit of the crew members who were in close proximity to me.

The leader of our team of creative eccentrics was producer Joy Flynn, now a young retiree who spent her entire career at KET. We almost lost Joy on one of our road show specials. She was on a high point looking at a scene with the videographer when she slipped on loose rocks and tumbled end over end down a mountain at Cumberland Gap. She was banged up and cut so severely she required a hospital emergency room visit.

Joy not only had to think about the production itself and the coming editing challenge, but how to keep us somewhat happy, too; making sure we stopped for lunch and dinner breaks, and listening to everyone's input, from where we ate to how a scene could be shot. Joy wasn't one of the high-strung personalities the television industry is infamous for. She was laid back, yet effective. She knew we worked harder if we had at least some ownership in the project. Yet, in the end, she got what she wanted out of the production.

You can live with your co-workers on the road in one of two ways. You can be unhappy and even hostile, or you can do the best you can at your job and laugh a lot. We chose the latter. We laughed at ourselves and we laughed at each other, as we rolled down the seemingly endless highway.

KENTUCKY SCENES

In the Bluegrass region of Kentucky, this weather vane is telling of the "all things horses" mentality of much of the population.

The architecture of the Shakers can be described as simple,
but their quality and craftsmanship are extraordinary.

In 1805, a religious group known as the Shakers established a settlement in Mercer
County. The Shakers were celibate and believed in a simplistic, hard-working way of life.
Today, Shaker Village at Pleasant Hill is a National Historic Landmark.

Thoroughbreds at Donamire Farm near Lexington take a break from grazing at the farm's traditional white, four-plank fences. One of the horses is shaking a fly off its nose.

They're off at northern Kentucky's Turfway Park. Kentucky is the "horse capital of the world," with nearly 250,000 horses of all breeds living in the state, along with equine and equine-related assets worth billions of dollars.

The seasons, people, and horses can provide postcard scenes during the Keeneland races in Lexington..

The author and Dr. Sandy Bates, at the most famous sporting event in the world, the Kentucky Derby.

Two young men hang tobacco in a Shelby County barn. The picture looks like it could have been taken 100 years ago because traditional methods of harvesting tobacco have changed little over the generations. Fewer crops are being planted as a result of the Federal Tobacco Buyout Program.

Bella, a spotted Great Dane, looks as though she's sharing a glass of wine with her friend Toby at a Kentucky winery. Vineyards and wineries are sprouting up in increasing numbers across the state, enough so that Department of Agriculture officials are calling it "explosive growth."

The Spanish-style Four Roses Distillery near Lawrenceburg was built in 1910 and is listed on the National Register of Historic Places. The distillery is open for tours and is part of the increasingly popular Kentucky Bourbon Trail.

Much like an old country store, the Binsini Fish Market in the little Mississippi River town of Hickman, Kentucky, is a gathering place and the site of many tall tales and outright lies.

Old country churches like Anderson County's Pigeon Fork Baptist Church still dot the rural landscape of Kentucky.

CLOSING THOUGHTS

When I retire from this unique occupation, I don't think I'll be able to go for long periods without getting in my truck and just driving. The winding road will stir memories of journeys and escapades, of stories that begged to be discovered. Every once in a while I'll need to wander aimlessly and re-live those crazy days of restless spirits, wheels, highways, and motion—motion we thought would never end.

It hasn't ended for me yet. Even though my broad-brimmed hats are getting dirtier and crumbled, even though I've lost too many canine sidekicks too quickly over the years, I'll keep going. Through books, magazines, and television, I'll gladly tell you the stories I found 'round the last bend. Stay tuned for volume two.

ABOUT THE AUTHOR

Dave Shuffett has been a popular television host and producer on both the regional and national levels for 25 years.

From 1989 to 1995, he served as host and producer of the long-running Kentucky Department of Fish and Wildlife television series, "Kentucky Afield." He then took his skills to the national level as owner and host of "Outdoors with Dave Shuffett," airing on broadcast stations and The Outdoor Channel. After three years of crisscrossing America, he returned home in 1999 to become host and segment producer for Kentucky Educational Television's (KET) weekly series, "Kentucky Life," replacing well-known storyteller, writer and television host Byron Crawford. Shuffett is still at the helm of the show, telling stories of the people and places that make Kentucky such a wonderful place. He is also co-host of the popular new KET series, "Kentucky Collectibles."

Shuffett is a nine-time Emmy Award nominee for on-camera performance and television producing and, in 2005, was the winner of a national Telly Award. He is a popular public speaker, integrating humor with stories of his adventures. He is also the bi-monthly "Great Outdoors" columnist and photographer for Kentucky Living magazine.

Shuffett was born and raised in south central Kentucky in the small town of Greensburg, county seat of Green County. He attended Murray State University and graduated with a bachelor's degree in communications in 1982. He has two children, Will and Miranda, who grew up watching their dad on TV and accompanying him on many adventures.